1 MONTH OF FREE READING

at

www.ForgottenBooks.com

By purchasing this book you are eligible for one month membership to ForgottenBooks.com, giving you unlimited access to our entire collection of over 700,000 titles via our web site and mobile apps.

To claim your free month visit:
www.forgottenbooks.com/free776794

* Offer is valid for 45 days from date of purchase. Terms and conditions apply.

ISBN 978-0-266-51619-4
PIBN 10776794

This book is a reproduction of an important historical work. Forgotten Books uses state-of-the-art technology to digitally reconstruct the work, preserving the original format whilst repairing imperfections present in the aged copy. In rare cases, an imperfection in the original, such as a blemish or missing page, may be replicated in our edition. We do, however, repair the vast majority of imperfections successfully; any imperfections that remain are intentionally left to preserve the state of such historical works.

Forgotten Books is a registered trademark of FB &c Ltd.
Copyright © 2017 FB &c Ltd.
FB &c Ltd, Dalton House, 60 Windsor Avenue, London, SW19 2RR.
Company number 08720141. Registered in England and Wales.

For support please visit www.forgottenbooks.com

Historic, archived document

Do not assume content reflects current scientific knowledge, policies, or practices

CATALOG
FROM
FITZGERALD'S NURSERY

FITZGERALD, Pro.

STEPHENVILLE,
TEXAS

R. F. D. 5

Fitzgerald's Nursery

J. E. Fitzgerald, Proprietor.

STEPHENVILLE, ERATH COUNTY, TEXAS, R. F. D. NO. FIVE.

INTRODUCTION

About Ourselves: We own an orchard here in Erath County. We have every variety of fruit or plant in bearing that we offer for sale. We have many kinds of peaches, plums, apples; and twenty-three varieties of Jananese persimmons. We know just what fruit will pay. It is no hearsay with us. We have made many mistakes we can tell you how to avoid.

Many nurserymen propagate and sell trees they never saw in bearing. At the proper season we can often send samples of the fruits we grow. We have been growing all kinds of fruit here for more than fifteen years, and got our education in the school of hard knocks. As to our responsibility we can refer you to the First National bank, the Farmers National bank, Cage & Crow bankers, any business house in Stephenville, or to the Stephenville Tribune, our leading newspaper.

It is impossible to estimate the value or profits of an orchard for home use; for aside from the money value, it is a great pleasure to have even a few trees in the back yard on a city lot. If you don't belive a man prizes them offer to cut one down. You'd have a row with the man of the house, the good lady, and on down to the least tot. When it comes to fruit for the market it depends on the man. One man can get more for a load of fruit than another. It is possible to make ten acres of fruit pay better than one hundred acres of cotton, and you set the price for your fruit.

We do not claim to send out the cheapest trees, but we believe our trees will pay the planter better than any cheap tree that can be bought. Our trees have been well tested and will bear. One tree that will bear you big crops of fine fruit is worth three that do not bear, or if they do bear, then bear fruit of inferior quality. Our advice is don't plant cheap trees as a gift. All fruit will be higher during the next few years than ever before. I contend that a good Elberta peach or a good plum tree is worth five dollars to the planter the day he sets it, and will be worth more money every year if well taken care of.

Orchards have died out all over the south, others have been neglected owing to the lack of help. It will pay you to plant an orchard this year.

PLANTS BY MAIL. Each year we send hundreds of plants by mail. In fact we make a specialty of this. We will mail roses and tree fruits at the each rate. Of course, we can't send large trees by mail.

ABOUT EXPRESS. Only under special agreement will we pay the express. But, if your order amounts to five dollars you can add fifty cents worth of trees and plants to your bill to help you pay the express. And if your order amounts to ten dollars, you can add one dollar's worth of trees and plants to your bill for express; and add one dollar for each additional ten dollar's worth ordered.

These offers do not apply to vegetables or potato plants.

MISTAKES. We make every effort to have every plant true to name, but the most particular will sometimes make mistakes, and for this reason it is mutually agreed between ourselves and our customers that we are to replace anything that proves untrue free of charge, and that we will be held responsible no further.

We begin shipping about November 15, and continue to ship berry vines until April 1. Trees are best planted during November, December, January and February.

THE COLD WATER POURER.

No matter where you live there is always some fellow ready to pour cold water on your plans; to say, "this is no fruit country." Up in Washington state, the finest apple country in the world, there are fellows going around saying, "this is no apple country." Up in New York state, where pears grow to perfection, some one is always saying, "this is no pear country." After you get a berry patch and the vines are literally loaded with big, black, luscious fruit, some fellow will come along; and after he has eaten about a gallon of your berries he will say, "this is no fruit country. Now, back yonder where I came from you could raise berries as big as goose eggs, and they tested better than these do here." But these fellows help you out, because they chill the timid fellow's plans to plant an orchard, and thus help you get a big price for your fruit. Maybe your place is not the best place in the world for fruit, but if you get a good price for what you do raise maybe you can make more money than the man who is raising fine fruit but has to sell it cheap.

It may strike you that my price list is mighty badly mixed up, and so it is. The truth is, I wrote it myself. I am no journalist; don't know much grammar; was educated in the school of hard knocks. I could have employed some man to write me a price list, but I preferred to write it myself, and tell what I learned about my plants in my own words. I have two nursery catalogues before me; one from an eastern nursery, another from a nursery in California. They both have the very same reading in them and the very same pictures. This shows that they were written by the same man. Maybe the man who wrote these catalogues could not tell a San Jose scale from a weed seed, nor an apple tree from a thorny locust. Very often the owner of a nursery lives in town. He depends on hired help to dig and pack your plants. This is the reason when an orchard comes into bearing you often do not have what you ordered.

A CHAPTER ON HOW TO PLANT

Every year I get about two hundred letters from people wanting to know just how to plant and what time to plant trees and vines.

From about October fifteenth to the middle of April will be a good time to plant. However, I always preferred November, December, January and February as my planting months. We always pack trees so they will reach you in the best shape. When they come if you are not ready to plant them right then it is a good plan to heel them out. That is, take all the straw from around the roots, untie the bundles and bury them out in good, moist soil. Wet the roots good with several buckets of water. Some people set them straight up when they go to heel them out, but I always lay them nearly down. They are not so likely to dry out if the moist dirt reaches nearly to the top.

When you go to plant trim off all broken roots. If you plant in the fall you can trim the roots back pretty close. When you set the tree, if it is one-year-old straight sprout it is better to cut it back to within eighteen inches of the ground. If it is a two-year-old, cut the limbs back to within half way to the body of the tree.

There is a great difference of opinion as to how far apart to set all kinds of trees and plants. Six feet apart each way is a good way to set blackberries. Then you can plow them both ways. Or make rows seven feet apart and set vines three feet apart in the row. Either way is satisfactory but they are harder to work the last way. Sometimes we set them between fruit tree rows. Say set them so they will be eight feet from the tree rows.

If you live where figs winter kill you can set the fig plants twelve feet apart each way. I like to set peach trees about twenty-five feet apart. Plum trees eighteen feet apart each way. Pear and apple trees from twenty-one to thirty feet. Such apples as Florence crab, Yellow Transparent and Duchess can be set fifteen feet apart each way, but the Yellow Transparent will grow up and make a large tree after a while.

Japanese persimmons can bet set fifteen or twenty feet. Grape vines are all right in rows twelve feet apart and different distances apart in the rows.

You can easily figure for yourself the number of trees to the acre. There are 43560 square feet in an acre. If you are going to set your trees twenty feet apart just multiply 20 by 20, this will give you 400. Then divide 43560 by 400. You will get the number of trees to the acre. If you aim to set your berries seven by three feet just multiply 7 by 3, which will give you 21; then divide 43560 by 21.

McDONALD BLACKBERRY.

Several years ago I bought one dozen plants of McDonald. These were accidentally planted through the middle of my Early Wonder berry patch. When these berries came into bearing they were the wonder of all who saw them. The plants had sent out runners fifteen feet long, and were almost ropes of berries to the end of the vines. I gathered five gallons of fruit from a single vine that sold in a local town at fifty cents per gallon. I got to figuring how many berries an acre would make with the plants set six feet apart, or twelve hundred and ten plants per acre. The next year I planted three acres of McDonald in a solid block, but when they came to bear they did not mature a berry. Something was wrong. I soon found that this berry must be planted near some other early bloomin gberry to pollenate it. Most all practical fruit growers know that it wont do to plant one variety of fruit in a solid block; but I was a new beginner. I now have six acres of McDonald and Early Wonder with a few Haupt and Rogers that I am really proud of. I doubt if there is another six-acres tract of land in this whole country that pays as wellas my Early Wonders and McDonald. Since finding out the great value of McDonald I have been advertising it in the north. I have sold thousands of plants and root cuttings to nurserymen all over the north. It is proving hardy as far north as Illinois, and on the Atlantic coast it bids fair to proving better than any berry so far found. It is fine in Georgia. One berry planter in that state wrote me that he would set two hundred acres, or enough so that he could ship a car load of fruit per day. McDonald is as large as the largest blackberry. The berries turn black several days before it is ripe. The berries will keep a week after being picked. This is the earliest and most productive blackberry known. I call it a blackberry, but it seems to b a cross between a blackberry and a dewberry. The vines are very vigorous growers. It sends up many canes from the roots that do their best when bearing time comes. Can be grown on a trellis or kept pinched back, as the grower prefers. I keep the plants pinched back. As intimated, I am the introducer of this plant to the north, and most all nu - serymen there got their original start from me. This is a berry that the man whon wants to make money growing berries cannot afford to overlook. On the other hand, the man in town can grow a dozen plants on the back yard fence and have plenty of berries to slpply his family.

If you plant McDonald this year you will have a prize well worth having; but be sure to mix a few Early Wonders in, as it will not bear when planted alone, and Early Wonder is needed in all fruit collections. It will pay well for its room.

Note—The McDonald picture appearing here is from berries grown by Prof. L. R. Johnson, Cape Girardeau, Missouri. The cut was made by the Rural New Yorker, and shows actual size of the berries. They grow well in Missouri.

Logan Berry: A cross between a black berry and a raspberry. In England this is said to be the most popular berry of all. It has the flavor of a raspberry, but the size and shape of a blackberry.

Plants 10c each, $1.00 per dozen, $5.00 per hundred.

Haupt Berry: This berry came from southern Texas. The originator claims this to be the largest, sweetest and most productive berry of all. It is large enough and productive enough, but the plants are mighty thorny. It pays better further south than it does here.

Improved Haupt: When the Haupt first came out there was a general mixture of plants. Some of them were entirely worthless. Among the mixup I found a plant that grew very thrifty and bore extremely large berries and lots of them. In fact it is one of the finest berries I know. I call it the Improved Haupt. It will pay you to plant a few of them. The picture on the cover of this catalogue is one vine of Improved Haupt. This berry will often make five gallons of fruit to a single vine.

Mammoth Blackberry: It is truly a Mammoth berry for they are an inch and a quarter long, and they are the best cooking berry I ever saw. I don't know why it is called blackberry, for its vines trail on the ground. I believe this wil prove fine in dry countries, for it is a wonderful drouth resister. The canes are not thorny enough to bother, and it is fun to pick the big black fellows. Very early and productive. Prices, 10c each; $1 per dozen; $500 per hundred.

Early Wonder Berry: A few years ago I grew the Dallas blackberry. It was very unsatisfactory. It did not bear enough and was too thorny. A neighbor had a berry that he said was Dallas that was far superior to my Dallas. At last I decided to get his plants instead of the Dallas I had. I have now been growing this berry for ten years. Everybody that saw it said it was the most wonderful producer they had ever seen. I had always been undecided as to which was the true Dallas. At last I sent to two reliable nurserymen for Dallas plants and got the same kind of plants I had at first. So, evidently my neighbor had some kind of berry heretofore unknown in Texas. For want of a better name I call it Eearly Wonder. And it is an early woider. This blackberry is nearly as large as the famous Austin dewberry. It begins to get ripe when the McDonald is half gone, and has ripe berries for five weeks. It is a fine combination berry with McDonald, and will produce at least three times as many berries as the old Dallas berry. It might be called an everbearing berry, for if the weather is favorable it will sometimes bear a light crop in the fall. It has fewer leaves than any other berry I have, and is always a delight to pickers. People who want berries for home use or to make berry juice cannot afford to overlook the Early Wonder. If you plant this berry and McDonald in combination you will have the most productive berries in the whole country. This berry will certainly give satisfaction to anyone who plants it. The seeds are very small. In fact, it is almost seedless. I have just received a letter from New Mexico, stating that Early Wonder has a nice fall crop. A letter from Washington state also says Early Wonder has a fine fall crop. Prices, same as McDonald.

Giant Mimalaya Blackberry: This berry is much advertised. It is very late, and on deep sub-irrigated land will bear often enormous crops. Where a man wants a few plants and can water them they are fine. Can be trained into an arbor, since the plants often make runners thirty feet long.

Mercerau Blackberry: By the time Jordan is gone we have Mercerau getting ripe. This is my last to ripen and my best late blackberry. I have later berries, but do not regard any of them near so good to pay as Mercerau. This berry came from New York state, and I find it is very difficult to propagate, therefore I must get a good price for the plants.

Jordan Blackberry: This is a late blackberry that is fine to prolong the season. It is very productive and is sweet as a berry can be. Here in Texas it begins to get ripe about the first of June.

Dallas Blackberry: A firm, mid-season berry. Jordan is a better berry.

Austin Dewberry: The practical berry grower, who grows berries to supply a home market needs fine berries from the very first of the season to the last. To supply an abundance of berries after Early Wonder is gone I know nothing better than the Austin dewberry. The plants are fine growers and the berries are very large. I have seen Austin berries nearly as large as a small hen egg. In south Texas they grow this berry to ship, but I consider it a local market berry. W. J. Shultz, a local planter of Brown county, Texas, says this berry never fails to pay him a hundred dollars per acre for his local market, but, of course, in our small western towns, our local markets are limited.

Lucretia Dewberry: This well known dewberry has never been grown much in Texas. I understand it does fine at Clyde, but for me it is not productive enough. The berries are not so large as Austin, but sweeter. Prices, same as Austin.

Several years ago I was peddling blackberries from a small spring wagon on the streets of Stephenville. A man came along on a load of hay with four mules to his wagon. He was away up in the air, and looked down on me and asked "if I didn't have mighty little to do?" I probably sold my load of berries that day for nearly as much as the man got for his big load of hay, and I had loads of fruit for many days of come. If you can make it a rule to sell as much as ten dollars' worth of fruit each day for six months out of the year you will beat a hundred acre hay farm; and you can raise the fruit on five or ten acres.

APPLE TREES.

I have spent nearly a life time raising apples here in Erath county. In this time I have learned that it pays to set the kinds that will bear the quickest. There are some kinds of apples that it will take the trees ten years to come into profitable bearing. I do not regard trees that it takes the best part of a man's life to bring into bearing as of much value, and especially if he can get trees that will bear in a few years. My apple trees are propagated from trees that bore in three or four years here in my orchard. If you get trees that will bear quick you will get your money back many times over before you will get even a crop from the slow-bearing kinds.

Yellow Transparent: A very large, clear yellow apple that begins to get ripe the first of June. The trees are rather dwarfish growers, but live a long time. On good soil they will finally make immense, compact trees. The trees begin bearing early, often the second year. The apple is a fine cooking apple, and always brings a good price on the market. When you plant your orchard be sure to include this tree.

San Jacinto: As I write this I have four of these immense apples on my desk that weigh two and a quarter pounds. You never saw a prettier apple in your life, and you seldom see a larger one. Here is an apple that you just can't afford to overlook.

Jonathan: This apple is so well known by all orchardists that it hardly needs a description. However, it is a fiery red apple. The trees are light colored. Bears every year here in the south.

Delicious: This apple is now famous for its quality the world over. It makes a firey, quick-growing tree that will grow most anywhere. These trees are inclined to be upright in growth. It comes into bearing very quickly and always bears big crops. But its crowning glory is its quality. Wherever planted it soon runs all other apples of its season out of the market when people get a taste of this magnificent apple. The apples are medium-sized, striped. If you have no Delicious apples in your orchard you are missing a good thing, and if you are planting an orchard be sure and do not overlook delicious. It gets ripe in August.

Kennard's Choice

Kennard's Choice: The first tree of Kennard's Choice is said to have been found growing wild in a thicket in Tennessee. The tree seems still to make good to grow under almost wild conditions, for it will grow where any tree will grow. This apple is very large, flat, red. Sometimes it gets so so dark colored as to be mistaken for Arkansas Black. It is a very abundant bearer of high quality apples. It should be in every orchard.

Lincoln: Here we have an apple that is said to do well even down on the coast. Thought to be a seedling of the Rhode Island Greening. Makes straight growing trees. The apples are greenish colored. Gets ripe in August. An abundant and prompt bearer. It ought to be tried in all southern states.

Winter Banana: Several years ago we ordered three trees of this remarkable apple by mail. When they reached us they were not much larger than a lead pencil. We set them out, and the third year after setting each tree bore several apples and have been bearing ever since. This is the apple that Andrew Carnegie paid twelve dollars a bushel for. It is a yellow apple, just the color of a banana. I believe it will bear quicker after being set than any other apple. The trees grow very rapidly.

Wine Sap: A late fall apple. This apple is rather small, but is fine quality and a sure bearer. It is well adapted to our Texas climate, but is better if planted on rather rich, moist soil. Then it is fine.

Crab Apples: We have found this one of the most profitable of tree fruits. Will grow anywhere plums will, bear big loads every year, nothing bothers the fruit, gets ripe in June, makes the finest of jelly, jam, preserves. These will take the place of plums to a great extent after they are known. This fruit should be planted 100 trees per acre, the trees bear two to three bushels to the tree at five and six years. The fruit has always sold so easily for me that I have been trying to contract with my neighbors to plant crab apple orchards. The contract price offered was $1.50 per bushel f. o. b. cars in bushel baskets. This looks like a good thing to the planter, but people are so slow to take hold of a new thing I have so far contracted for only one small orchard. I find that a good ad in any of the big daily papers will sell hundreds of bushels of crab apples and the price I usually get is $2.50 per bushel. (Oct. 8th, have just returned from Fort Worth and found there Crap Apples selling for $5.60 per bushel.)

VARIETIES

I am offering only two varieties:

Florence: Gets ripe in June. Bears very abundantly. Trees bear second year after setting. The best of all crabs.

Transcendent: Makes a very fine tree. Good for shade. Bears heavy after trees get old. On deep sand this tree will make a shade tree that can not be beaten for beauty.

SHADES

We have a nice stock of the following shades, ranging from one to five feet: Umbrella China, Pecan, Wild Persimmon and Black Locust.

MULBERRIES

Mulberries bear abundantly and are fine for chickens. There is little difference in the trees. Hicks and black English are probably the best.

COMPASS CHERRY

The only cherry that will bear in the south. A cross between a cherry and a plum tree.

JAPANESE PERSIMMONS.

A few years ago I made the statement that a Japanese Persimmon orchard would beat an orange grove. That seemed rather a broad statement at the time I made it, but it is fast proving to be a fact. Most people think that a Jap persimmon is like the old wild persimmon we used to have in the old states. The fact of the business is that the Japanese persimmon is as large as an orange, In fact I have on my trees now Hyakune persimmons that will weigh a pound. I now doubt that there is any fruit tree anywhere that will pay as well as persimmons properly taken care of. They stand more drouth than any other tree and are sure to make a crop every year. The persimmon is one of the most delicious of all fruits. I sell thousands of them for invalids. At the same time they are the most beautiful of all fruits. The man who plants a persimmon orchard now will in a few years be getting returns on his land greaer than he ever got before. Don't listen to the man who says, "persimmons grew wild where I came from." He don't know what he is talking about. But if you have a piece of good land, plant it to persimmons. And persimmons will grow on most any kind of land. Take good care of your trees, and in five or six years, when your trees go to bearing, watch your neighbors go persimmon crazy. I will say this: When I set my first persimmon orchard lots of my neighbors thought it was a joke. But the joke has gone the other way. I am what you might call a persimmon crank. At the same time I know a good thing when I see it. plant all the persimmons you can. They will make you independent. I can certainly back up what I say about persimmons. I sell them to bankers, merchants, and everybody else here in Stephenville. They can tell you how quickly I can sell a load of persimmons. After people once learn them they are the most saleable fruit of all. They are in a class by themselves.

Every man who has a persimmon tree wants more. Ask the man who has a Japanese tree what he thinks about them. I will say this, however, there are some varieties that fail to bear here in the south. In setting your trees you had best set the kind that you know will bear. You will make no mistake to set Tamopan, Eureka and Hyakune. But you will make a mistake if you don't set them.

Eureka Persimmon tree in bearing in my orchard.

HOW TO PLANT PERSIMMON TREES.
(This also applies to pecans.)

Do not let the rotts be exposed for a minute to the dry air. I use a post hole digger. Dig a hole a fraction deeper than the tree grew in the nursery. After the tree is set pack the dirt thoroughly around the roots. In fact tamp it. Then cut the tree to within eighteen inches of the ground. Now take a spade and make a mound of dirt around the tree nearly to the top. Let this mound gradually wear away through the summer. If you will be careful with your trees you can get them every one to live. The third year they will begin bearing a little. From then on they will never miss a crop.

Description of Varieties.

Eureka: Here is a persimmon that originated here on my place seventeen years ago. I have sold thousands of the trees. It makes a very symetrical growth, the leaves being very large. The fruit is very large tomato shaped— the most beautiful of all persimmons, being deep red several days before ripe. You cannot plant anything finer. Has stood the cold in Missouri.

Tampopan: This persimmon came from China. Every one has a ring around it. The tree grows very rapidly and makes a fine shade tree. It is said to grow seventy feet high in China. It is a good one to plant.

Hyakume: I know one at Handly, Texas, on a dry, rocky hill, that is a beauty, and was loaded with fruit nearly as large as teacups when I saw it in October. It was fine.

Tane Nashi: Large acorn-shaped. Not good as the others on account of lack of color.

In addition to the above varieties I have many others, but the ones I mentioned are proving best for me.

THE PEAR

Garber: The Garber is the earliest. The trees grow very fast The leaves are dark green and will make a fine shade for any yard or lawn. The fruit is large. The pear is rather flat at the blossom end. This pear with me begins to get ripe about the first of August. The quality is very good; and sells readily as an eating pear. Yellow and showy.

The Keiffer: The Keiffer pear begins to ripen in September. It is very large, but must be stored before it is good to eat. This is the great preserving pear here in Texas. The trees, and at least the fruit will stand more rough treatment than any other pear. This is often called the pear of plenty, and it well deserves its name. You can plant a Keiffer pear tree in any odd place and it will always pay for its room. Mr. R. Tyndall of Clairette,

Texas, has a Keiffer pear tree in a hard back yard that bears every year. Last year this tree bore thirty bushels of as fine pears as ever grew, and brought Mr. Tyndall $1.00 per bushel. Mr. Tyndall told me of this pear himself and would not trade his tree for a good horse. If well cared for a Keiffer tree will often live fifty years. Yet you can buy a little tree almost for a song.

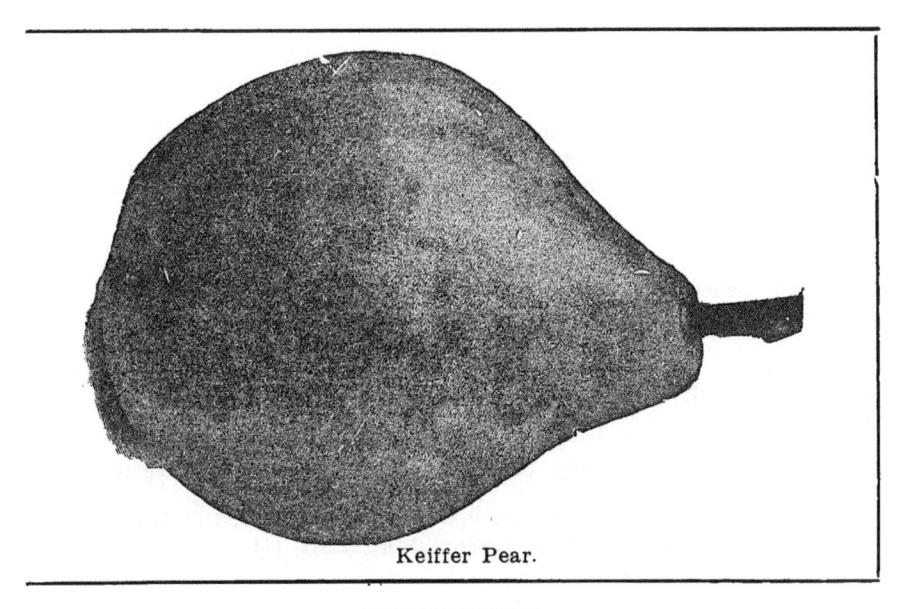

Keiffer Pear.

PEACH TREES

Don't crowd your peahc trees on your land and they will bear more regularly for you. I like them set from twenty-five to thirty feet apart each way. The peaches I list below are described in order of ripening, as near as possible.

Mayflower: Positively the earliest peach in the world. Makes a very good tree, and bears lots of peaches. The peaches are red and are fine quality for such an early peach. A very profitable peach to plant for market.

Victor: Second early; fine tree and tolerable good fruit.

Sneed and Triumph: These two peaches do not amount to much.

Arp Beauty: Makes a good tree. The finest quality of all peaches. I doubt that there is a better eating peach than Arp.

Early Wheeler: This peach is proving to be one of the greatest money makers of all peaches. It is an early peach, and at the same time a canning peach. But its immense size and high color is what makes it sell better than all other peaches. You can't go wrong to set an orchard of Wheelers.

Carman: A big white semicling peach. Very fine quality and a sure bearer. Gov. Hogg and Mamie Ross are about the same as Carman.

Belle of Georgia: Another big cream and crimson peach. An excellent shipper and soft and luscious when ripe.

Chinese Cling: An old, old peach. Everybody knows it. Very large.

Old Fashioned Cling Peach: This is the old Indian peach that was raised in this country forty years ago. The trees are very thrifty and are a certain crop. If you want the old Indian peach here it is.

White Heath: Also called White English. A very fine large pure white September peach. One of the finest of all fall peaches. We raised some here in Erath county this year that were simply perfection.

Henrietta: A big yellow cling stone peach that simply never fails to bear. This Early Wheeler and White Heath and Elberta are my favorite market peach.

Stinson October: A very late Heath. Always pays and sure to bear.

This list of peaches includes all that we have found best by test. But we can supply you Early Elberta, Lemon Cling, Late Elberta, Elberta Cling, Niagara and Crawford's Late.

Elberta: The Elberta is still a standard tree, and has made more money for peach planters than any other peach tree. This year's trees of this peach are very scarce, and all kinds of substitutes will be sold by nurserymen. If you set the Elberta be sure and get the genuine

Augbert: Just an August Elberta, and one of the finest of all big yellow freestone peaches.

Late Elberta: Another fine yellow peach that ripens in August.

PLUMS

We have every plum we list growing and fruiting in our orchard. We have several other varieties, but these we consider best to plant.

Omaha: Trees look like the wild plum trees that grow in the wooded sections. Plums are very large and very fine. Gets ripe the first of September. Blooms out late. Trees grow to be large.

Burbank: Limbs of this plum are often carried around by agents to show what wonderful bearers the trees are. A large reddish yellow plum. Fine for cooking.

Botan: Large, red sweet.

Poole's Pride: One of the best July plums.

Wild Goose.

Gold: July, very fine.

Wickson: Very large free stone plum. In places not subject to late frost, this is fine.

Milton: Early red, sure to bear. Of the same character as Wild Goose.

America: Large yellow, sure bearer. I believe America will bear more bushels than any other plum. Every man planting a commercial orchard needs America.

Golden Beauty: A yellow September plum.

A NEW APRICOT

The general objection to apricot trees is that they do not bear. There are thousands of trees sold every year that never do bear, but accidentally I have found one that will bear every time. If you will plant this apricot you will soon decide it is worth more than a carload of the never bearing kind of trees. Price of small trees $1.00 each. We have only a few of these trees that run about three feet. They are worth five dollars each for any yard.

Cluster: A sure bearer and early.

Moore Park: It is becoming very popular.

We can make special prices on large quantities of apricots as well as peaches and plums. Write us if you are planting a large orchard.

THE FIG

It has long been thought that figs could not be raised in this part of Texas, but it has now been found that they could be raised as far north as New York. I have two acres of figs. There are no two acres on my place that pay any better. Have my fig plants set twelve feet apart each way. Each plant makes from one to two gallons of figs a year. I have more than three hundred plants to the acre, and as figs sell readily at 40 cents per gallon, they pay pretty well. They are easily cultivated and are a sure crop. But it must be remembered that my figs frost bite down to the ground every year and sprout up from the ground to bear. If they are given some winter protection so the plants will not winter kill the above yield can be doubled. My fig plants will bear the first year after being set.

Magnolia: A rapid growing forked leaf fig. New set plants will bear the first year. Figs are large, straw colored. This as well as my other varieties will make a most delightful pot or house plant in the north. If set in the garden and given some winter protection they will be a delight to the grower and a curiosity to all who see them.

Ischia: A vigorous growing fig. Ornamental. The fruit is light green outside and right bright red inside. It has a delicious sweetness hard to describe.

Brunswick: Trees fast growing. Leaves large, ornamental. A large, black fig. Grows about as large as an ordinary hen egg.

Hirtu Japan: This is a dwarfish growing fig. Makes a fine pot plant. Figs are rather small, dark brown. Ths is a very abundant bearing fig. The little trees not over six inches in height will begin bearing.

The fig is a mildly laxative. The grower can get almost any price for fresh figs. Eat figs and throw physics to the dogs.

If you live in town and have only a small lot, plant a few grape vines, a dozen McDonald and Early Wonder berries and two or three fig trees. If the soil is good plant three or four persimmon trees. They will grow in a very small space and you will have one of the most ornamental trees you ever saw. The finest peaches ever grown in Erath county were grown in a small back yard, where the ground was nearly as hard as a brick. The apricot makes a fine back yard tree. It delights in hard soil, and bears hig crops some years.

THE PECAN

A pecan orchard is the best life insurance in the world. I know men who have paid insurance for a few years and then let the insurance lapse. If these same men had have planted pecan orchards they never would have lost them. They would have been there probably two hundred years to be paying dividends. In fact a pecan tree seldom dies. They make the best shade trees. Plant them instead of the shade tree. Young man, if you are just starting out in life be sure and plant a few pecan trees. You will never regret it. When other things fail they will keep you on your feet. The trees should be set from forty to sixty feet apart. If given real good cultivation our quick bearing trees will begin bearing some nuts in five years. By the time they are seven years old they will bear ten pounds to the tree and at ten years old will be bearing fifty pounds. The idea is to cultivate the trees so as to make them grow an inch in diameter each year. If you live in a pecan country you probably know wild pecan trees that bear as high as six hundred pounds to the tree. A twenty-year-old tree of such as Stuart ought to do nearly this well. I claim that two good pecan trees would be worth as much as a paid up life insurance policy for $1,000. A pecan tree owned by a Mr. Moore in Lampasas county, bears 1,000 pounds per tree and sells at 50c per pound.

Another tree owned by the same Mr. Moore bears 600 pounds at a time. These sell at from 50 cents to $1.00 per pound. Here are just two pecan trees that could not be bought for $5,000.

Our trees are budded from the best bearing trees. Dug with long tap roots. A pecan tree never will bear until it forms a good tap root. Some nurserymen cut the tap roots to make the trees form side roots. They claim they live better, but if our trees are planted deep in the ground, say three and a half feet, they will stand the drouths better than these lateral rooted trees and will bear three years quicker. Nature knows what kind of roots she wants on her trees.

Varieties of Pecans We Offer.

Stuart: Large, run as high as two inches long. Tolerably soft shell, very fine quality. Trees very beautiful quick growers. Bears abundantly. Considered about the best pecan.

Burkett: A large, round pecan. Trees bear quickly. Fine.

Halbert: Grows fine on upland. A small pecan from west Texas that will bear nearly as quick as a peach tree.

Schley: Said to be the premier pecan. Large, long. Trees slender growers.

We also have Texas Prolific, Delmas, Pabst, Moneymaker and Success. These all good.

Pecan bud Wood: We can furnish pecan buds to bud over other trees at $3.00 per hundred. Budding is best done during April, May and June. We can often send a man to bud the trees for you who knows how the work is done.

GRAPES

This fruit dates back as far as time itself. In fact it was one of the first fruits man ever knew. It is the only fruit that men can practically live on and never tire of it. In southern Europe the peasants practically live on grapes and black bread and they live longer than any other people. There have been more books written on grape culture than on all other fruits combined. All of us remember when we were boys how we roamed the creeks hunting for the wild grapes. Some people imagine grapes are hard to grow. They can be grown cheaper than any other fruit. If your grape vines have died or you have made a failure in planting grapes don't give up, plant a few of our new vines. I was in a vineyard near Ft. Worth a few weeks ago that has yielded the owner more than two thousand dollars per acre for the last four years. This may seem unreasonable, but when you figure that a good grape vine will bear fifty pounds and better to the vine and the owner had three hundred vines per acre, also he sold all his grapes for fifteen cents and better per pound.

John Burrough, the famous naturalist and bird lover, made his fortune growing grapes. Another good point about grapes is that they can be grown on the edge of a desert. Grapes like dry weather and that is the kind we have here in the south mostly.

If you do not know how to grow grapes write to the department of agriculture, Washington, D. C., and they will send you books on grape growing, or I can send you a book for $3.50 telling you exactly how to grow this fruit. Go into the grape business, plant several acres and you will not regret it. There is the biggest demand for grapes now that has ever been in the history of the country.

The Deleware Grape: The carliest of all grapes. Red; makes a very slender, weak growing vine. Should be planted seven or eight feet apart.

R. W. Munson: Very large early, black grape. Has strong growing vine and should be planted at least twelve feet apart. The leaves are very large and make a beautiful arbor grape.

Niagara: The large, white grape that is much raised over the country. The vines bear very abundantly for a few years then play out. Why not plant grapes like Carman and Virginia Dare that will live and bear a life time.

America: An early, black grape. Vines are hardy, live for years. This grape must be planted near some other kind or it will not bear.

Beacon: Another very large, black. Fine vine that lives a long time.

Concord: This grape originated about one hundred and fifty years ago. The grapes are large and black, has a strong, foxy flavor. Bears pretty well for a few years, but all the grapes do not get ripe on the cluster at once.

The Carman Grape: Vines very thrifty, in fact, just as hardy as vines can be. No insect ever bothers them. Will grow on any kind of soil. The grapes are large and thick on the cluster. In fact, a cluster of these is solid nearly as a ball. Bears from one to two bushels per vine and the best eating grape I ever saw. If you have been planting grapes that would not sell plant some Carman. They outsell anything else on the market.

The vines will live from twenty to fifty years. Plant twelve to fifteen feet apart in the rows.

The Carman grape begins to get ripe about August 10th, and will hang on the vines after getting ripe for several weeks.

Virginia Dare: Here we have one of the most vigorous growing grape vines of the south. I have had shoots from one of these vines to grow thirty feet in a single season. I believe if one of these vines were planted near a building 100 feet high it would grow to the top of it. This grape is related to the mustang grape but all the hot burny taste has been bred out of it and we have left one of the most delicious of all grapes. The grapes are large, dark red. The juice is red. This is probably the heaviest of all grapes. A single bushel, if heaped, will weigh sixty pounds. The vines are very productive, and will make as high as four bushels to the vine. If you want a grape arbor plant two of these and two Carman grapes. In field culture the vines should be at least fifteen feet apart and twenty feet is not too far.

Champanel: This grape is the best of all grapes for limy, hard, black soils. In fact, it will grow practically anywhere. Grapes large, black. Plant twelve feet apart.

Marguerite: A very late grape. This is of the fox grape family. In fact, it is only an extremely fine wild grape of North Texas. Plant twelve feet apart.

ROSES.

Our roses are the finest field-grown plants. They will begin blooming almost immediately after being set.

We have pink and white Killarny; Marchiel Neil, Etoyle de France, Augusta Victoria, Dorothy Perkins and others. In fact, we have all the leading roses.

Asparagus Roots

Barr's Mammoth, Conover, Palmetto and Colossal asparagus.

SPECIAL OFFERS

Special Number One: For $2.00 we will mail you three Austin dewberry plants, three McDonald, three Eearly Wonders, three Rogers, three Jordan and three Haupt. This will give you a chance to plant some of the best berries.

Special Number Two: For $2.00 we will mail you three Wine Sap apple trees, three Loncoln, three Jonathan and three Kennards. Just right for a small orchard.

Special Number Three: For $2.00 we will mail you three Niagara grapes, two Concord, three Magnolia figs, and one Ischia fig. You can have your own fig trees for a very small price.

Special Number Four: Three to four foot trees. Three Victor, three Mamie Ross, three Carmen, three Henrietta and two Stinson. A whole peach orchard for only $6.00. By express.

Special Number Five: Two Burbank, two Botan, two Shiro, two Golden Beauty, and two Milton plums, all for $6.00.

Special Number Six: Four Keiffer, four Garber pears; one Yemon, one Hyakume, one Tane Nashi and one Eureka persimmon, all for $4.00.

VINES.

Honeysuckle: A beauitful, well known vine. Loved by every one. 50c each.

Clemattis: A rather rare vine. Bears just simply a mound of white flowers. Something beautiful. 50 cents each.

Kudza Vine: I do not doubt that our strain of this vine is the most wonderful, fast growing plant in the world. If planted on good soil it will cover dwelling in a single season. It is useful as well as ornamental. Stock like to eat the vines and if planted along a terrace the terrace will never break. Will stop up any kind of a ditch. Every farmer should have a start of this plant. Something of the nature of a bean vine and will enrich the soil. Be sure you include a plant or two of this in your order. 15c each, $1.25 for 10; $10 per 100.

Dorothy Perkins Rose: I am often asked what will cover up an old fence and make a pretty hedge. This rose will do it and will if planted in rows about six feet apart make you as prety hedge as you ever saw in your life. The plants are healthy, and grow in the hardest soil. I will sell you plants cheap, and they are certainly worth planting. I have the pink and white, however, I prefer the pink. 20c each; $1.50 for 10; $15.00 per 100.

SHRUBS

Althea: A well known old shrub sometimes called Rose of Sharon. 35c each.

Crape Myrtle: We have only red and pink of this beautiful shrub. 35c each.

Pomegranate: A shrub that has been known for thousands of years. Mentioned by King Solomon. Bears large, red flowers and an Edible fruit. Ornamental and stands the hottest weather and grows in the hardest soil. 35c each; 10 for $3.00.

Spirea Van Houtte: Also known as bridle wreath. Bears a mound of white flowers in early spring. Makes a good hedge or is fine to plant next to a building. Always used in landscape gardening. 25c each; 10 for $3.00.

Salvia: Small growing shrub about two feet high. Deep red flowers. Stands drouth. Fine for edging. 25c. each.

Tamarix: Another shrub or tree that stands drouth. Makes a fine shade if pruned right on the hardest land. Pink blooms. 25c each.

Bush Honeysuckle: A small ornamental tree.

California Privett: A well known hedge-in plant. You can see them in all towns.

Figs For Hedges: If planted, say three feet apart, and kept trimmed right, the fig makes a pretty and interesting hedge plant.

FRESH FRUITS IN SEASON.

During the summer we can fill orders for peaches, plums, grapes, persimmons, pears, apples and crab apples. Write for prices.

AMERICAN HONEY PERSIMMON SEED

Several years ago a man in Illinois sent me some seed of what he said was the finest wild persimmon in the world. These are large, very sweet, stand drouth and make a fine, fast growing tree. Some of the trees will have leaves nearly as large as the magnolia leaves. Very ornamental. A tree of this will not bear if alone. The persimmons are liked by pigs, chickens, and to tell you the truth, you will have a hankering to visit the trees. They begin to get ripe the first of September and continue all the fall. I have no trees to offer, but will send a packet of fifty seed for fifty cents. Plant them any time during the winter, about three inches deep. These persimmons are so much better than the old wild persimmon that you can seel them on the market. The seed are sure to grow. Plant them around the house or in the field for shade, for the chickens, for the children, for the wife and the boss. In a few years you will say that you never invested fifty cents better in your life.

CHINESE DATE OR JUJUBE

Makes a tall growing tree with light green leaves. Fine for shade and bears very abundantly of brown fruits about the size of the little finger. Will make more chicken and hog feed than any other tree. Is interesting and a profitable tree to plant.

ARBORVITAES

It has always been considered that the arborvitae is the most difficult of all plants to transplant. If the roots are never allowed to get dry they are about as easily transplanted as peaches or apples. I will take special pains in digging these. We will keep the roots from exposure at all times and pack well. Never unwrap them until ready to set. Then see that the roots are not exposed for a minute to the air. I have Rosedale, the prettiest of all arborvitaes.

OKRA SEED

It is peculiar but true that okra seed are the most difficult to get true to name. For several years I have been ordering White Velvet okra, but only recently got the seed true to name. As a vegetable okra is one of the best crops a market grower can produce, and the genuine White Velvet will make twice as much as any other kind. I have saved several bustels of seed from my market garden, and can offer market gardeners genuine White Velvet. this okra is very early, and the pods stay tender for quite a while. If you are going to plant okra it will pay you to get the genuine White Velvet. Price of seed: Small packet 5 cents; ounce 10 cents; pound, 50 cents.

OLD FASHIONED CORNFIELD BEANS

Years ago we raised a bean here in this country that made more to the acre than any other bean. I had lost seed of them until a few years ago I sent to a man in Georgia and got some of the same seed. These are vine beans, but will make all right without stakes. They bear immense crops of the finest of all beans—large, meaty fellows, that bring the highest market price. Why raise poor beans when you can raise this one? Be sure and get a start this year. Beats the Pinto bean. Price per ounce, 25 cents; per pound, 75 cents.

We want the plants we sell you to be sure and grow. Your success means our success, and for that reason we agree to replace al that die within one year at half price. But we hope you will take good care of your trees and not lost many of them, for your loss means our loss. If they are damaged when you get them from the railroad be sure and notify us at once and we will take the matter up with the company. Remember, we waive all responsibility if you do not notify us at once; but if notified within five days we will replace the shipment.

WHERE BERRIES AND FRUIT TREES WILL DO WELL

Every year I get letters from people asking, "Do I reckon berries will do well with them?" They say that "no one raises them in their country." I wish to state that the blackberry will grow well on most any kind of good oat, corn or cotton land. If no one raises berries where you live, this is a good reason why you ought to give them a trial. An old man once gave me this advice: He said, "Joe, don't never waste your time trying to figure out why a black hen lays a white egg, but get the egg." The thing to do is give them a trial. Get the egg before the other fellow finds the nest.

Twenty-five years ago Capt. J. R. Ellis, our pioneer apple grower of this country decided to grow apples. He ordered several hundred trees and set them out. His neighbor thought it was funny for a man to be trying to grow apples this far south. But when Mr. Ellis' apple orchard got to bearing people went twenty miles to see it and buy apples from Mr. Ellis. Capt. Ellis has made a fortune from his orchard. He got the eggs before the other fellow even found the nest.

Not only this, but Capt. Ellis has come very near finding the foundation of youth; for he is one of the youngest old men I ever saw. He can do as much work as any young man. Fruit growing is his hobby, and he has no time to think of growing old.

Men who have such pleasant hobbies as growing fine fruit do not get old as fast as men who have nothing to do but count their money and whittle goods boxes.

I like to visit Mr. Ellis and his orchard. Though he has a thousand, he knows the name of every tree by the color of its bark. He can tell you when each tree was set, its fruit record, and whether it bears paying crops or not.

Great things are made up many small things. Even the mighty clouds that pass over the earth are made up of many drops of rain. When you start to market if you load your wagon with many small things, all taken together may some day amount to enough to buy a farm or an automobile. A few gallons of blackberries; a bushel or two or apples or pears, a few plums, taken to town when you go will pay expenses. If you have no time to plant a berry patch let your wife plant one. Maybe when she sells enough berries to buy an auto she will let you ride in it occasionally.

Eat Fruit! Lock the medicine closet and lose the key. A dime's worth of good, ripe Japanese persimmons is worth a quarter's worth of pills.

FITZGERALD'S NURSERY, STEPHENVILLE, TEXAS, R. F. D. 5

Vigo Park, Texas, Feb. 8, 1919.
Mr. J. E. Fitzgerald,
Stephensville, Texas.
Dear Sir:—
Enclosed find check for $20.00. Please send me the following: * * * *
I ordered plants from you once before and was well pleased with them. I want to put out an orchard this fall and I intend giving you the order. At what price will you furnish an assortment of trees for an acre?
Please send the plants by express to Tulia, Texas, and write me when you ship as I live 30 miles from Tulia.
Very Truly Yours,
I. K. Curry,
Vigo Park, Texas.

Security, Texas, June 17, 1920.
Mr. Fitzgerald,
Stephenville, Texas.
Dear Sir:—
What will you charge me per 1,000 for McDonald and Early Wonder berry plants this fall or winter, good strong plants?
The Early Wonders I got from you are 3 to 1 ahead of the Dallas I have.
Yours Truly,
C. W. Langridge.

Decatur, Ga., Jan. 29, 1921.
Fitzgerald Nursery Co.,
Stephencville, Texas.
Gentlemen:—
Please send me catalogue and price list as I want some more Black Berries.
Sold my farm, have to start over again. The berries I got from you three years ago are fine. Early wonders and McDonalds do well here.
Yours Respectfully,
John Keller,
Decatur, Ga., Route 3.

Hico, Texas, Nov. 23, 1920.
Fitzgerald Nursery,
Stephenville, Texas.
Dear Sir:—
Enclosed find check for $2.45 in in payment of a small order for fruit trees.
Mr. Simmons has recommended you to us and I trust to receive strong and good trees.
Since I do not know how much the shipping will be you may have that collected here or send me bill for same. I am handing your catalog and price list to a neighbor who has a large order to fill.
Thanking you for prompt attention,
Respectfully,
Mrs. V. F. Weiser.

Meers, Okla., Feb. 19, 1921.
Dear Mr. Fitzgerald:—
The trees came Monday and were the best packed trees I ever received. Am greatly pleased with them. Thanks for the extra tree, the Cooper's early apple. If it is the same as the Cooper's early white that I had in Kansas 35 years ago I will sure prize it very highly as that was a very fine cooking apple and a young bearer. I had a small tree of it only 2 years planted that had 65 fine apples on it.
Sincerely Yours,
E. T. Daniel.

Dublin, Texas, March 15, 1921.
Mr. J. E. Fitzgerald,
Kind Sir:—
The bill for the trees is so much less than I expected that I am enclosing you a check for the entire amount. Please accept my thanks for your kindness and be assured that if in the future I desire more trees I will certainly call on you for them.
Yours Respectfully,
W. F. Hart.

Greenville, S. C., Feb. 6, 1921.
Fitzgerald Nursery,
Gentlemen:—
I notice your ad in Cutheators. I purchased some black berry plants from you a few years ago. They are fine. Send me some of your catalogues. Send one to Mrs. J. T. West, Greenville, S. C. and one to Mrs. J. W. Moon, Greenville, S. C., both on Route 6.

J. M. Blakely.

Smyrna, Ga., Feb. 11, 1919.
Fitzgerald Nursery,
Stephensville, Texas.
Dear Sir:—
I am enclosing postoffice money order for $5.00 and 25 cents in stamps for which send me by parcel post the trees and plants as per enclosed order. I am anxious to try out your plants and trees as if they do well in this sectin, I will set out a good many. Kindly let them come forward as soon as cnvenient.

I was just talking to a man from your section and ht said you had probably not continued in the nursery business as everybody out there was talking oil and digging for oil just now but I told him I had just received your 1919 catalogue and guessed you were still in business.

With best wishes, I am,
Very Truly,
H. Konigsmark.

Fort Worth, Texas, June 3, 1921.
J. E. Fitzgerald,
Stephensville, Texas,
Dear Sir:—

In spite of the two frosts and two freezes we sold over $800.00 worth of berries besides what we gave away and used for ourselves.

I feel sure I can give you the names of several who want your berries this fall. Your berries will sell its lf, it doesn't need a salesman.

I am awfully proud of our berry patch and want to put out more berries.

I always am glad to recommend it. If you can find time to come up here I feel sure you will be well paid as the biggest berry man in the country told Mr. King he wanted your berry for next year.

I want some fruit trees, will be glad to see you at your earliest convenience.

Am still working for the same Railroad but want to be able to quit by fall.

The last time I heard from you you were to come by here after visiting your daughter in a hospital. Trust you and yours are enjoying the best of health, I remain.

Very Respectfully,
Mrs. J. E. King,
Box 193, Handley, Ft. Worth Texas.

Trustworthy Trees & Plants
MEMBERS AMERICAN ASSOCIATION OF NURSERYMEN

Lightning Source UK Ltd.
Milton Keynes UK
UKHW012329061118
331891UK00010B/1012/P